# Cowboy Slang

# for Modern Day Use

## VOL. II

### Ricky Adams

# Cowboy Slang
## for Modern Day Use
## VOL. II

Ricky Adams

Published by Cowpoke Press
TikTok @cowboyslang



ISBN: 979-8-3302-5716-4
Printed in the United States of America
1st Edition

# MORE COWBOY SLANG

Saddle up, partner, and learn some cowboy slang. Were you aware that cowboys in the 1800s had a distinct slang all their own? Most of these words have vanished from the English language. It's about time we start including these back into our everyday conversations. Impress and amaze your friends, family, and colleagues with your new wild west talk. You can tap into the essence of a character from your favorite cowboy-themed video game or simply add some grit to your everyday chats. Developing fluency in cowboy slang will elevate your authenticity and reveal your true inner cowboy.

# Alfalfa Desperado

-Farmer-

"I prefer to get my lettuce at the Alfalfa Desperado's market on Sundays."

# Backdoor Trots

## -Diarrhea-

"Bro, that philly cheese steak destroyed me. I've had backdoor trots for days."

# Balderdash

## -Nonsense-

"I tried reading the instructions to put together the cabinet, but it was straight up balderdash! I'm not even sure what language it was in."

# Bazoo

## -Mouth-

"The date was fine, but he chews with his big ol' bazoo open. That was a big turn off. I could see that he doesn't fully chew his steak which means, to me, that he'll never finish anything all the way."

# Bee
# Sweetening

## -Honey-

"This tea is a little bland, you got any bee sweetining?"

# Beetle-crushers

## -Feet-

"That girl never wears shoes. Boy, I tell you what, she's going to need to wash those beetle-crushers before she steps foot in my house."

# Belly Wash

## -Weak coffee-

"Nah I prefer pour over coffee, everything else just taste like belly wash to me now."

# Chaw Up

## -Finish up-

"Can you chaw up that burger so we can get going? You've been eating it for over an hour…"

# City Slicker

## -A person from the city-

"Sorry I'm a certified city slicker and don't know much about how to work these tractors."

# Cookie

## -A Chef

"Excuse me waiter, can you please send my compliments to the Cookie on this here delicious liver and onions."

# Cow Juice

## -Milk-

"Ok, this guy needs a cow juice and crullers STAT!"

# Cow Sense

## -Smarts-

"That girl has cow sense. I still don't get how she made an omelet in the microwave."

# Cut Dirt

## -Run-

"I've never seen Joe cut dirt like that. He was so embarrassed he had to get out of there quick."

# Dabster

## -Expert in everything-

˝My brother, the dabster, can figure out anything. He got hired by some fancy tech company in high school, well that is until they found out he was 14.˝

# Dilly-Dalling

## -Delaying-

"Would you quit your dilly-dalling and just finish the assignment so we can go get burritos. I'm starving."

# Down to the Blanket

## -Pretty much broke-

"My last pay check only lasted me about 3 days, and now I'm down to the blanket. So anyways honey… I'll need you to cover dinner tonight."

# Feller

## -Fellow-

"Dude, I'm not sure. Why don't you go ask that feller over yonder. He might know where the snow cone stand is."

# Fish or Cut Bait

## -Walk the talk-

"Yeah, yeah, you've told me a million times about how you can do a kickflip. Well you have your board so fish or cut bait…let's see it.

# Get the Mitten

## -Rejected by a crush-

"I don't know if I'll ever recover. I love Karen, but when I told her how popping I thought she was she gave me the mitten."

# Go Boil Your Shirt

## -Get lost!-

"Dude, I already said I don't want you buying me a drink. Go boil your shirt...I'm not interested!"

# Grab a Root

## -To eat a meal-

"I'm not sure how you think we'll be able to drive all the way to that pizza place and grab a root in 30 minutes. It's like 15 miles away, and we already clocked out for lunch."

# Hang Up One's Fiddle

## -Give up-

"My wife really wants to go to Hawaii, so I need to just hang up my fiddle and buy the tickets. I still think Costa Rica would be better."

# Hankering

## -Wanting-

"I have a mighty strong hankering to go to that concert, but the tickets are so gosh darn expensive!"

# Hearty as a Buck

## -Healthy-

"The doc asked me how I'm feeling. I told him I'm hearty as a buck. He was not amused."

# Helter-skelter

## -Hurry-

"Man I wish you could have seen Tim last night, he ran all helter-skelter up to this girl and she had zero interest. It was great."

# Higgledy-Piggledy

## -Confusion-

"That guy back there was making no sense. He sure must be higgledy-piggledy to believe all that about Area 51."

# Hill of Beans

## -Worthless-

˝I swear this degree in Anthropology is a hill of beans when you're trying to get a regular job out of college. Maybe I should just be a young professor or something. ˝

# Hobble Your Lip

## -Shut up-

"Oh hobble your lip dude, you know you have no rizz."

# Honey-Fogle

## -To cheat-

"Well I got an A on that test because I totally honey-fogled it. I had the answers written on my arm. I missed one though because the ink smeared towards my elbow."

# Hornswoggle

## -Tricked-

"Welp, I straight up got hornswoggled. This is not a real 1st edition holo gem collector's card. It's just some knock off."

# Illy

## -Sick-

"Sorry boss I'm all illy today, I can't come in for my shift. Pretty sure I have that dolphin flu everyone has been talking about.

# Iron Horse

## -Train-

"Sorry I'm late boss. I missed my iron horse this morning. I got there just as it was leaving the station."

# Jawing

## -Chatting-

"Our teacher was getting upset because we were all just jawing up a storm instead of working on our projects."

# Jump the Broom
## -Get married-

˝Maybe one day I'll jump the broom, but for now I'm happy with just living life to it's fullest, and seeing where the universe takes me.˝

# Marble Orchard

## -Graveyard-

"I know the rent is cheap, but I just can't live next to a marble orchard. The vibe and the view is just awful."

# Mashed

## -In love-

"I haven't seen him in a bit. He's mashed to some girl he met online, but I'm pretty sure it's just an Ai bot."

# Painting the Town Red

## -Having a blast in town-

"Last night's scavenger hunt was wild! We really painted the town red, and left no stone unturned. "

# Pitch a Fit

## -Temper tantrum-

"Listen, I'm sure they'll eventually fill the ball pit back in at the jungle gym. No need to pitch a fit about it. Plus those ball pits are pretty gross."

# Pokey

## -Jail-

˝Nah, we stopped doing that duct tape in the street prank when we accidently got a cop car. He chased us and threatened to throw us in the pokey. It was hella traumatic.˝

# Roper

## -Confident person-

"It's fun going to the casino with Bill. He's a roper for sure at the dice games, although he did loose 20k last time we went. I swear the dealers know him by name now."

# School Ma´am

## -A woman school teacher-

"Miss Flowers was the best school ma´am out of our whole school. She had these funny shoes she would always wear, but boy was she rough on my English lessons."

# Simon-pure

## -To be truthful-

"Karen, are you being simon-pure with me right now? There's no way your hairstylist suggested that cut?!"

# Some Pumpkins

## -A big deal-

"Listen that report was no joke, it was some pumpkins. I barley got any sleep this past week."

# Tenderfoot

## -New to the job-

"Anywhoo, Jim asked me to make a thousand copies of this flyer, which would have taken forever, so I asked the tenderfoot to do it instead. He's probably been at the copier machine all day."

# Ten Commandments

## -Fingers-

"Hey, keep your ten commandments out of the peanut butter jar! We all eat from it, that's disgusting."

# Tombstones

## -Large teeth-

"You see the tombstones on that chihuahua back there? I'd steer clear of it if I were you."

# Yammerin'

## -Talking-

"If you quit you're yammerin' maybe we'd be able
to hear the movie."

# Yonder

## -Off in the distance-

"Pretty sure the pie shop is just over yonder. I can't wait for a slice of lemon meringue."